Created by RC Kids at
Rivers Crossing Church in Mason, OH.
Copyright © 2024

To request permissions, contact the publisher
at rckids@riverscrossing.com

ISBN: 979-8-9895404-0-2
First paperback edition January 2024.

AUTHORS:

Andrea Goslee, Alexandria Taylor,
and Rebecca Conner

ILLUSTRATORS AND DESIGN:

Madison Keil
and Bekah Reed

Scriptures taken from the Holy Bible, New International Reader's Version®, NIrV® Copyright © 1995, 1996, 1998, 2014 by Biblica, Inc.™ Used by permission of Zondervan.

Parents,

We're so glad you've chosen to walk alongside your child on their baptism adventure! In this resource, you'll find practical questions to guide them as they decide to follow Jesus and get baptized. Before you talk to your child about their next step, read the ABCs of Salvation on the following page. Once you finish, do the following:

1: **Find a quiet place to sit together with your child.**

2: **Read the book *Maya and River's Campout Adventure* together.**

3: **Start your adventure by asking your child the questions beginning on page 4 and completing the action steps. You should work through one page each time you read *Maya and River's Campout Adventure*.**

NOTE: Follow your child's cues to know the best time to talk. Are they attentive and excited? Are they restless and asking to do something else? Are they asking additional questions about their faith? As you take these cues, you will know when they are ready to move on to the next page and which faith steps to take.

4: **Continue your adventure by doing one or more of the following:**

- Lead your child in the salvation prayer.

- Sign up your child to get baptized.

- Choose ways to help your child continue their adventure with Jesus.

Connect with a church leader if you have questions throughout this journey together. We're excited to see how your child continues to grow in their faith through Baptism Adventure!

Blessings,

The RC Kids Team

rckids@riverscrossing.com

ABCs OF
SALVATION

Before starting the adventure with your child, take a moment to review the ABCs of salvation for yourself. No matter who you are or what's in your past, you are created in God's image and likeness. God desires a relationship with you. But sin has created a barrier between you and God – just as it has for the rest of humanity.

> *"It's your sins that have cut you off from God. Because of your sins, he has turned away and will not listen anymore."*
>
> Isaiah 59:2

THE GOOD NEWS IS THAT RESTORING YOUR RELATIONSHIP WITH GOD IS AS EASY AS THE ABCS

A. **Admit that your sins have caused you to fall short of God's holy standard–that you can't save yourself, but need a Savior.**

> *"For everyone has sinned; we all fall short of God's glorious standard."*
>
> Romans 3:23

B. **Believe that God sent Jesus as our only hope for salvation.**

> *"For this is how God loved the world: He gave his one and only Son, so that everyone who believes in him will not perish but have eternal life."*
>
> John 3:16

C. **Choose to receive Jesus into your life, placing your faith in Him as your Savior and following Him as your leader.**

> *"But to all who believed him and accepted him, he gave the right to become children of God."*
>
> John 1:12

START YOUR ADVENTURE

Talk through the ABCs with your child by asking them the following questions from *Maya and River's Campout Adventure*. You can work through one section of questions each time you read the book. Move through this guide at a pace that is comfortable for your child. It's okay if you don't ask every question.

A. ADMIT

Admit that you do wrong things and need Jesus to help you.

Maya and Benny made a mistake since they didn't tie a knot in the rope, so River got lost in the woods.

- What is the difference between making a mistake and doing something wrong?

- What did Maya do wrong when she realized River was missing? What could she have done instead?

- When we do bad things, that is called a sin. Have you ever done something wrong? How did you feel?

> Even if we try our best, we all do wrong things. When you do bad things, it is called a sin. You can tell Jesus the truth by admitting what you did wrong and asking Him to forgive you.

The friends decided to help each other look for River.

- How did they help each other?

- Who are some people that can help you?

- Who can help you learn more about Jesus?

> God sent Jesus as the Savior of the world to help you and save you from your sins. Jesus is always there to help you when you ask Him. Just like Jesus helps you, He wants you to help others, too!

5

Maya went to Nico for help when she realized River was lost.

- Who can you talk to when you do something wrong and need help?

- What would you like to talk to Jesus about?

You can always ask Jesus for help. He won't be upset with you, even if you do something wrong. Jesus loves you no matter what!

ACTION STEP

Write down some things you have done wrong. Say a prayer to ask Jesus to forgive you for each of these things.

6

B. BELIEVE

Believe that Jesus died on the cross and came back to life to forgive you.

Maya says she will do whatever it takes to find River. That's how God feels about us!

- How did Maya feel when she lost her dog, River?

- Have you ever lost something? How did you feel? If you found it, how did you feel then?

- Maya loves River so much! Name one person that you love. How can you show love to them?

Jesus loves you so much that He died on the cross to forgive you. He wants you to believe in Him so He can be your friend forever!

Maya believed they would find River, even though it was getting dark and they couldn't see a way to cross the creek.

- It's sometimes hard to believe in things we can't see. Do you believe in Jesus even though you can't see Him?

Faith is believing in something we do not see. Hebrews 11:1 says, "Faith is being sure of what we hope for. It is being sure of what we do not see."

Maya confesses to Gramps that she lied to Him.

- Does Gramps forgive Maya even though she lied to him?

- Do you believe Jesus still loves you even when you do wrong things?

When you do something wrong, you should ask Jesus to forgive you. When you believe in Him, He forgives you because of your faith and belief in Him and because He loves you very much.

Throughout the story, Gramps keeps an eye on the kids in the woods. Eventually, they needed his help to rescue River.

- How many times can you find Gramps following along in the woods? (4)

- Have you ever tried to do something on your own that you couldn't do?

- Did anyone help you when you couldn't do it by yourself?

You can't get to heaven on your own. The only way to get there is through a relationship with Jesus. You have to decide to follow Jesus. When you believe in Him and ask for forgiveness, you can start a relationship with Him so you can someday live in Heaven with Jesus forever.

ACTION STEP

Read and memorize the scripture John 3:16 (NIRV)
"God so loved the world that He gave His one and only Son. Anyone who believes in Him will not die but will have eternal life."

C. CHOOSE

Choose to follow Jesus and live your life for Him.

Maya and her friends enjoyed spending time together at the campout.

- What were some things Maya and her friends did together?

- What do you think makes a good friend?

- What are some things you and your friends do together?

- What are some things you can do with your friend Jesus?

> When you choose to follow Jesus and live your life for Him, He will always be with you. He wants to spend time with you and to be your friend forever.

Maya said that River is the best gift anyone has ever given her.

- Have you ever received a special gift? What was it, and how did you feel when you received it?

- Jesus is the best gift ever! Have you asked Him to be your forever friend?

> God sent Jesus to the world as His perfect Son to save us from our sins. Jesus is the best gift! The great news is when you choose to follow Jesus, you can't lose this gift. He will be your friend forever.

In the woods, while they searched for River, the kids had to choose which way to go.

- One choice you can make is to say yes to Jesus. If you have, how can you live your life for Jesus?

- If you haven't made that choice, you can say the salvation prayer on the next page and make that choice today!

It's up to you to make a choice to follow Jesus. It's the best choice you will ever make! Living your life for Jesus includes spending time with him and learning more about Him.

Nico realized that even with the compass, there were too many choices, and he chose the wrong path.

- How do you feel when you make the wrong choice?

- How do you feel when you make the right choice?

- Are you ready to make a choice to follow Jesus today?

There is only one way to get to heaven. It is by choosing to have a relationship with Jesus. So, choose to follow Jesus and live your life for Him!

ACTION STEP

Choose how you will continue your adventure with Jesus! Would you like to say the salvation prayer? Are you ready to get baptized? Review ways to spend time with Jesus and share your faith on page 19–20.

SALVATION
PRAYER

You can say this prayer with your child to invite Jesus to be their friend forever:

Dear Jesus,

Thank you for loving me. I admit that I do wrong things and need your help. Please forgive me for the wrong things I have done. I believe that you died on the cross to forgive my sins.

You came back to life so one day I can live in heaven with you. Today, I choose to follow you and live my life for you as my forever friend. I'm thankful you are my friend and will always be there for me.

In your name, I pray,

Amen

TIPS FOR PARENTS

- Work through the ABCs of salvation and the actions steps prior to saying the salvation prayer with your child.

- Choose a special place to pray together.

- Ensure that the decision to say this prayer comes from the child.

- Include other parents/family members to say the salvation prayer with you if your child is comfortable.

- Celebrate with your child once they make the decision to say this prayer and make Jesus their forever friend!

**YOUR ADVENTURE
CONTINUES...**

Has your child made a decision to follow Jesus? Have they intentionally prayed for Jesus to be their friend forever? Congratulations! It is an exciting time for your family, and we can't wait to celebrate together. (If your child hasn't made a decision yet, invite them to pray the salvation prayer with you on the previous page when they are ready). Here are some ways to help your child continue their adventure with Jesus.

GET BAPTIZED!

After we choose to follow Jesus, the Bible tells us to get baptized. Baptism is a public celebration of your child's decision to follow Jesus. Your child will be lowered under the water to symbolize their sins being washed away. Then, they'll be lifted out of the water to symbolize the new life they will live with Jesus. Learn more about baptism on the following page.

"What are you waiting for? Get up and be baptized. Have your sins washed away by calling on the name of the Lord."

Acts 22:16

BAPTISM

Is your child ready to get baptized? If so, congratulations! If you're still unsure, walk your child through these follow-up questions. If your child's answers align with the answers in parenthesis, that's a good sign that they're ready for baptism!

QUESTIONS TO ASK YOUR CHILD

- Write down the date you decided to follow Jesus.

- Who are some people who helped you learn about Jesus?

- What did Jesus do on the cross for you?
  (died and came back to life to forgive our sins)

- What is a sin?
  (the bad things we do that keep us from God)

- Why do you love Jesus?

- If you could share anything you want with your friends about Jesus, what would you say?

- Why do you want to get baptized?
  (because I want everyone to know that I am a follower of Jesus)

*NOTE

Many kids mistakenly believe that baptism is the same as making a decision to follow Jesus. Baptism doesn't save us. Our decision to follow Jesus is what saves us. Once a child has decided to follow Jesus, the next step is to get baptized and let everyone know they are a follower of Jesus.

SPEND TIME
WITH JESUS

The decision to believe in Jesus is the beginning of a relationship with Him. You'll want to spend time with Jesus each day like you do your closest friends. Here are some ideas of things you can do to connect with Jesus and grow in your faith.

PRAY

- Take a prayer walk.

- Find a special place in your house to talk to Him.

- Listen to hear what Jesus wants to say to you.

- Talk to Him at mealtime or bedtime.

WORSHIP

- Find a song about Jesus that you like to sing.

- Listen to songs about Jesus while you do one of your favorite activities.

- Listen to songs about faith in the car.

JOURNAL

- Find a notebook and write prayers to Jesus.

- Draw pictures describing why you love Jesus.

- Write out a favorite scripture verse and color it.

READ YOUR BIBLE

- Read your favorite Bible story.

- Memorize a verse from the Bible.

- Read a Bible story to a sibling or parent.

SHARE
YOUR FAITH

When we choose to follow Jesus, we should want to tell everyone we know about Him! Here are some ways you can share your faith.

SHARE WITH YOUR WORDS

- Invite a friend to church.

- Tell a friend about Jesus.

- Share your favorite Bible verse with a friend or family member.

SHARE WITH YOUR ACTIONS

- Help a neighbor.

- Smile and say hello to someone new.

- Do something kind for a friend.

- Help your family by doing extra chores.

SHARE YOUR RESOURCES

- Use your talents to make a gift for someone.

- Offer your time to serve other people.

- Earn extra money to help someone in need.

- Give a tithe (10% of the money you are given) to the church.

WRAP UP YOUR ADVENTURE

Congratulations on walking through these faith conversations with your child! One of the most important decisions your child will ever make is to follow Jesus. When they do, they will have a forever friend to talk to who will guide them as they live their life for Him.

Now, decide together with your child next steps to take. Review the previous pages or the list below to help them decide what to do next.

Do they need to pray to accept Jesus as their forever friend?

Are they ready to get baptized?

How can they spend time with Jesus?

- Pray
- Worship
- Journal
- Read the Bible

How can they share their faith?

- Words
- Actions
- Resources

As your child continues on this faith journey, remind them that it isn't a one time decision. This is the beginning of a great adventure where they'll get to know Jesus more and more each day. It will be the adventure of a lifetime!

Do you or your child still have questions or need help? Connect with your local church or another family member that has a relationship with Jesus for answers.

FOLLOW US ON SOCIAL MEDIA

@RIVERSCROSSING

@RIVERSCROSSINGKIDS